COMPUTER

SELF HELP TRAINING GUIDE

vol.1

A comprehensive and simplified step by step guide to computer appreciation with practical approach For Colleges and secondary schools

Benjamin Alex

Table of content

Introduction

In today's rapidly evolving world, computers have become an integral part of our daily lives. From personal and professional use to advancements in science, technology, and communication, computers play a vital role in shaping our modern society. Understanding the basics of computers is not only relevant but also empowering in this digital age.

At its core, **a computer is a device that processes and stores information**. It can perform various tasks, from simple calculations to complex data analysis, all in a fraction of the time it would take a human. What makes computers truly remarkable is their ability to execute repetitive tasks with incredible speed and accuracy, freeing up human beings to focus on creative and critical thinking.

But how does a computer work beneath its sleek exterior? What components make it function? How does it process and manipulate data? These are questions we will delve into as we embark on this introduction to the world of computers.

In this book, we will explore the fundamental concepts of computer science, including hardware, software, data representation, and more. We will unravel the mysteries of computer languages, programming, and algorithms, allowing you to gain a deeper understanding of the science behind computers and their applications.

Additionally, we will examine computer networks, the backbone of modern communication, and learn about the principles and practices of computer security to help protect valuable information in our increasingly interconnected world.

Whether you are a curious beginner or someone seeking to expand their knowledge in the field of computers, this comprehensive guide will provide a solid foundation. By the end of this journey, you will have a clearer understanding of how computers work, enabling you to harness their power effectively in various aspects of your personal and professional life.

So, let us embark on this exciting exploration of the world of computers, where technology meets innovation, and possibilities are limitless. Get ready to unlock the wonders of this ever-evolving realm and discover the amazing potential that lies within the realm of computers.

Basics of computers and their components

Computers are electronic devices that process and store data.
They operate based on instructions given by users and perform various tasks.
The following are some of the fundamental components:

1. **Hardware**: Computer hardware refers to the physical components of a computer that you can touch. Some key hardware components include:

    A. **Central Processing Unit (CPU):** Also known as the brain of the computer, the CPU executes instructions and performs calculations.

    B. **Memory**: Computers have two types of memory – RAM (Random Access Memory) and storage devices like hard drives or solid-state drives (SSDs). RAM stores temporary data that the CPU needs for quick access, while storage devices store data even when the computer is turned off.

    C. **Input devices**: These include a keyboard, mouse, and other devices that allow you to give instructions or input data to the computer.

    D. **Output devices:** Examples include monitors, printers, and speakers that display or produce the results or information processed by the computer.

2. **Software**: Computer software consists of programs and instructions that tell the computer what tasks to perform. There are two main categories:

    A. **Operating System:** The operating system (e.g., Windows, macOS, Linux) manages computer resources, runs applications, and provides an interface for users to interact with the computer.

    B. **Applications**: These are specific programs like web browsers, word processors, or graphic design software that perform particular tasks.

3. **Data**: Data is any piece of information that a computer processes, stores, or retrieves. It can be text, numbers, images, audio, or video. Computers use binary code – a system of combining 0s and 1s – to represent and process data.

4. Input and Output: Computers receive input through input devices, such as a keyboard or mouse. Users input commands or data, which the computer processes. The processed information is then displayed through output devices like monitors or printers.

5. Processing: The CPU performs calculations and executes instructions stored in memory. It carries out logical and arithmetic operations, making decisions based on given inputs and instructions.

6. Storage: Computers store data using various types of storage devices. Hard disk drives (HDDs) and solid-state drives (SSDs) are commonly used for long-term storage. They retain data even when the computer is turned off. Cloud storage and external drives are other options for storing data.

7. Networking: Computers can be connected together to form a network. Networks enable the sharing of data, resources, and communication between computers. The internet is a vast network of interconnected computers worldwide.

8. Peripherals: Peripheral devices are additional components that connect to the computer to enhance its functionality. Examples include printers, scanners, webcams, and external storage drives.

9. Troubleshooting: While using computers, problems may arise. Basic troubleshooting involves identifying and fixing issues like software errors, hardware malfunctions, or connectivity problems. This often requires understanding the computer's components and troubleshooting techniques..

Types of Computer Systems

There are several types of computers, each designed for specific purposes and varying in terms of size, processing power, and functionality. Here are some common types of computers:

1. **Personal Computers (PCs):** Personal computers are the most familiar type of computer used by individuals for general-purpose tasks. They come in desktop and laptop form factors and are typically used for activities such as web browsing, word processing, multimedia consumption, and gaming. PCs run operating systems like Windows, macOS, or Linux.

A desktop Computer

A laptop Computet

2. **Workstations**: Workstations are high-performance computers designed for specialized tasks that require significant computational power, such as computer-aided design (CAD), video editing, scientific modeling, or animation. They often have multiple processors, large amounts of RAM, and advanced graphics capabilities to handle demanding workloads.

workstation computers

3. **Servers**: Servers are computers dedicated to providing services to other computers or users over a network. They are optimized for reliability, security, and scalability. Servers can handle tasks such as hosting websites, running databases, managing email, or serving as the backbone of cloud computing infrastructures.

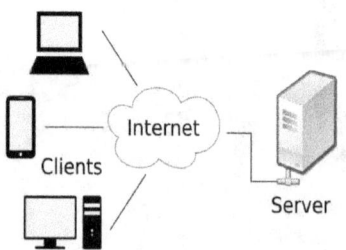

4. **Mainframes**: Mainframe computers are large-scale, high-performance systems capable of processing massive volumes of data and supporting thousands of users simultaneously. They often power critical applications in industries such as banking, finance, airlines, and government. Mainframes provide robust reliability, availability, and security features.

Mainframe computer

5. **Supercomputers**: Supercomputers are the most powerful computers, capable of processing complex scientific calculations and simulations at extraordinary speeds. They are used for tasks like weather forecasting, modeling nuclear reactions, drug discovery, and aerospace research. Supercomputers consist of thousands or even millions of interconnected processors, offering massive processing power.

Supercomputers

6. **Embedded Systems:** Embedded systems are specialized computers designed to perform specific functions within larger systems or devices. They are often embedded in everyday objects such as cars, appliances, medical equipment, or industrial machinery. Embedded systems are optimized for efficiency, reliability, and low power consumption.

Embedded systems

7. **Smartphones and Tablets:** Smartphones and tablets are portable computing devices that combine features of a PC, phone, and multimedia player. They have significant processing power, touchscreen interfaces, and access to a wide range of applications. Smartphones and tablets run mobile operating systems such as iOS or Android.

Smartphone and Tablet

8. **Wearable Computers**: Wearable computers are small computing devices worn on the body, such as smartwatches or fitness trackers. They are designed for tasks like health monitoring, fitness tracking, notifications, and limited interactions. Wearable computers often rely on wireless communication and have sensors to collect data from the user.

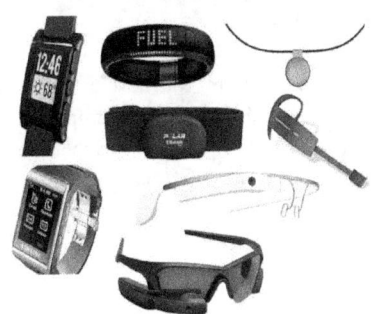

Wearable computers

Introduction to operating systems

An operating system (OS) is a crucial piece of software that manages and controls the hardware and software resources of a computer system.
It acts as an interface between the computer's hardware and the applications or software running on it, facilitating their communication and coordination.
The primary function of an operating system is to provide a user-friendly environment for users to interact with the computer. It provides a graphical user interface (GUI) or a command-line interface (CLI) through which users can execute commands, run programs, access files, and perform various tasks.

Operating systems also handle essential tasks such as managing memory, allocating system resources, scheduling processes, handling input and output operations, and providing security and protection for the computer system.
Furthermore, the operating system enables multiple applications or processes to run simultaneously by managing the allocation of CPU time and memory space. It prevents conflicts between different programs and ensures efficient usage of system resources.

There are various types of operating systems, including Windows, macOS (formerly OS X), Linux, Unix, and mobile operating systems like Android and iOS. Each operating system has its own distinctive features, design principles, and compatibility with different hardware and software.

Additionally, operating systems provide a platform for developers to create applications, as they provide a set of APIs (Application Programming Interfaces) and libraries for software development. These APIs allow developers to access various system resources and services, such as file management, network connections, and device drivers.

Different types operating systems (OS)

There are several types of operating systems, each with its own characteristics and designed for specific purposes. Here are some of the most common types of operating systems:

1. **Single-user, single-tasking**: This type of operating system allows only one user to perform one task at a time. It is commonly found in older computers and some embedded systems.

2. **Single-user, multi-tasking**: This type of operating system allows a single user to run multiple applications or tasks simultaneously. Examples include Windows, macOS, and Linux.

3. **Multi-user**: A multi-user operating system allows multiple users to access and utilize the computer system simultaneously. These systems provide features like user accounts, file permissions, and network capabilities to support concurrent access. Examples include Linux distributions used in server environments.

4. **Real-time**: Real-time operating systems are designed for applications that require precise and immediate response times. They are used in industries such as aerospace, industrial automation, and robotics.

5. **Network**: Network operating systems are designed to manage and coordinate multiple computers connected in a network. They enable sharing of files, printers, and other resources among networked computers. Examples include Windows Server and Novell NetWare.

6. **Mobile**: Mobile operating systems are designed specifically for smartphones, tablets, and other mobile devices. They provide specialized features such as touchscreen interfaces, app stores, and location-based services. Examples include Android and iOS.

7. **Embedded**: Embedded operating systems are used in specialized devices and equipment, such as digital cameras, routers, and point-of-sale terminals. They are typically lightweight, efficient, and tailored for specific hardware requirements.

8. **Distributed**: Distributed operating systems are used in environments where multiple computers work together to perform a task or share resources. They enable distributed computing and parallel processing, allowing tasks to be divided among multiple machines.

9. **Virtualization**: Virtualization operating systems, also known as hypervisors, manage and run virtual machines (VMs) on a single physical computer. They enable the consolidation of multiple operating systems on a single hardware platform, improving resource utilization and flexibility.

Functions of Operating Systems (OS)

The operating system (OS) performs several functions to manage the hardware and software resources of a computer system.

Each function plays a vital role in managing and coordinating the various components of a computer system to ensure its smooth operation and enable users to perform tasks effectively.

Here are some of the main functions of an operating system:

1. **Process management**: The OS manages and oversees processes, which are running instances of programs. It allocates system resources, such as CPU time and memory, to different processes, and ensures they run efficiently without interfering with one another.

2. **Memory management:** The OS is responsible for managing the computer system's memory. It allocates and deallocates memory to different processes, tracks memory usage, and provides mechanisms for managing virtual memory, such as paging and swapping, to optimize memory utilization.

3. **File system management**: The OS manages the storage and organization of files and directories on storage devices. It handles tasks such as creating, deleting, and renaming files, as well as managing access permissions, directory structures, and file metadata.

4. **Device management**: The OS interacts with various hardware devices, including input/output devices, storage devices, and networking components. It provides drivers and interfaces to enable communication between applications and hardware devices, manages device queues, and handles input/output operations.

5. **User interface**: The OS provides a user interface that allows users to interact with the computer system. This can be a command-line interface (CLI) or a graphical user interface (GUI). It handles user input, displays output, and facilitates user interactions with applications and system settings.

6. **Security:** The OS implements various security measures to protect the computer system and its resources. It controls user access levels through authentication and authorization mechanisms, enforces privacy and data protection policies, and detects and mitigates security threats, such as malware and unauthorized access attempts.

7. **File system protection**: The OS ensures that data stored on the file system is protected from accidental or intentional corruption. It performs file system checks and repairs, implements file permissions and access controls, and provides backup and recovery mechanisms to ensure data integrity.

8. **Networking:** The OS provides networking capabilities to enable communication between computers and devices in a network. It includes network protocols, drivers, and utilities to support tasks such as network configuration, data transmission, and network resource sharing.

9. **Error handling:** The OS detects and handles system errors and exceptions, such as software crashes, hardware failures, and resource conflicts. It provides error messages, logs, and diagnostic tools to help identify and resolve issues.

10. **Resource allocation and scheduling**: The OS optimizes resource allocation and scheduling to ensure efficient utilization of system resources, such as CPU, memory, and disk I/O. It uses algorithms and policies to schedule processes, allocate memory, and prioritize tasks based on factors like priority levels, deadlines, and fairness.

Differences Between Windows, MacOS and Linux Operating Systems

Windows, macOS, and Linux are three popular operating systems that have distinct differences in terms of their user interfaces, software compatibility, customization options, security, and pricing. Let's explore these differences in detail:

User Interface:

Windows: Windows has a user-friendly interface characterized by a taskbar, start menu, and a graphical user interface (GUI). It provides a consistent and familiar experience across different versions.

macOS: macOS offers a sleek, modern, and visually pleasing interface with a dock at the bottom of the screen. It is known for its intuitive design and ease of use, especially for creative tasks.

Linux: Linux provides multiple desktop environments (e.g., GNOME, KDE) that offer various user interfaces. It offers flexibility for customization and allows users to choose layouts, themes, and workflows as per their preferences.

Software Compatibility:

Windows: Windows has the widest range of software compatibility and supports a vast number of commercial applications and popular games. It is the most compatible platform for mainstream software.

macOS: macOS has a good range of software compatibility, particularly with creative tools and applications. However, it may have limited compatibility with certain specialized or niche software.

Linux: Linux has a growing software ecosystem, but it may have limited support for mainstream commercial software and games. However, developers and open-source enthusiasts benefit from a vast range of development tools and software options.

Customization Options:

Windows: Windows provides several customization options, including personalizing the desktop, themes, fonts, and colors. Users can also modify the taskbar and start menu to suit their preferences.

macOS: macOS offers some customization options, but they are relatively limited compared to Windows. Users can customize the desktop background, icon sizes, and choose from predefined themes.

Linux: Linux is highly customizable, allowing users to tailor almost every aspect of the operating system. Users can choose different desktop environments, modify window managers, and change themes.

Security:

Windows: Windows faces more security risks due to its popularity and widespread use. Despite consistent improvements in security features, it is more vulnerable to malware and viruses. Regular updates and third-party security software are necessary.

macOS: macOS has a reputation for strong security. It benefits from the closed ecosystem of Apple devices and their strict control over software distribution. However, it is not invulnerable, and users should still exercise caution.

Linux: Linux is known for its robust security and stability. The open-source nature allows for quick identification and mitigation of security vulnerabilities. While malware targeting Linux is relatively rare, it is not completely immune.

Pricing and Licensing:

Windows: Windows is a commercial operating system and generally requires purchasing a license. Different editions, such as Home and Pro, have varying costs. However, Microsoft provides regular updates and support.

macOS: macOS is exclusively designed for Apple hardware and comes pre-installed on Mac computers. It is not available for other manufacturers' devices, and updates are typically free.

Linux: Linux is predominantly free and open-source, allowing users to download, distribute, and modify the operating system without cost. Numerous Linux distributions are available, each with its own support and update policies.

There are many other differences, such as hardware compatibility, gaming support, and community support; however, these are some of the primary distinctions between Windows, macOS, and Linux. Each operating system has its strengths and weaknesses, and the choice depends on user preferences and specific requirements.

Computer Hardware

Computer hardware refers to the physical components of a computer system that are tangible and can be touched. These components work together to enable the computer to perform various tasks and processes. From the processor to the memory, storage devices, input/output devices, and other peripherals, computer hardware plays a fundamental role in the overall functionality and performance of a computer system.

These Components includes;

The heart of a computer system which is the central processing unit (CPU), also known as the processor. It is responsible for executing instructions and performing calculations. It consists of various components such as the arithmetic logic unit (ALU), control unit, and cache memory.

The Memory is another key component of computer hardware. Random Access Memory (RAM) provides temporary storage for data and instructions that are actively being used by the CPU. It acts as a bridge between the processor and the storage devices, allowing for faster data retrieval and execution.

Storage devices, such as hard disk drives (HDD) and solid-state drives (SSD), are used to store data and programs permanently. These devices provide long-term storage for operating systems, applications, files, and other data. They differ in terms of speed, capacity, and reliability, with SSDs generally offering faster performance and better durability.

In addition to the CPU, memory, and storage devices, computer hardware also includes input and output devices. These devices allow users to interact with the computer system. Common input devices include keyboards, mice, scanners, and microphones, which enable users to input data and commands. Output devices, such as monitors, printers, and speakers, display or produce information generated by the computer system.

Other important components of computer hardware include the **motherboard**, which serves as the main circuit board connecting all the components, and the power supply unit, which provides the necessary electrical power to the computer system.

With the rapid advancement of technology, computer hardware continues to evolve, becoming faster, more powerful, and more efficient. As new technologies emerge, such as solid-state drives, graphics processing units (GPUs), and peripheral devices, the capabilities and possibilities of computer hardware expand, shaping the future of computing.

The internal components of a computer

The internal components of a computer refer to the hardware components that are housed within the computer case or tower. These components work together to enable the computer system to function properly. The main internal components of a computer include:

1. **Motherboard**: The motherboard is the main circuit board of the computer system. It provides the platform for all other components to connect to and communicate with each other. The CPU, RAM, storage devices, and other peripherals are attached to the motherboard.

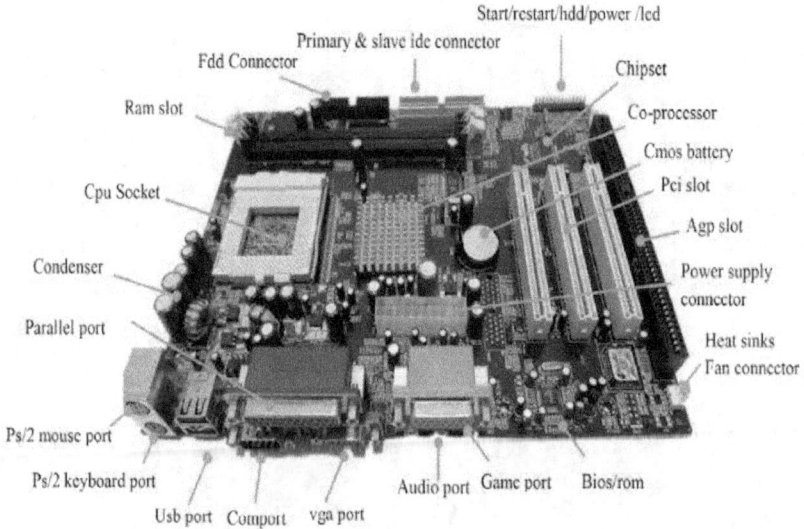

Motherboard

2. **Central Processing Unit (CPU)**: The CPU, also known as the processor, is the brain of the computer. It carries out instructions and performs calculations. The speed and performance of the CPU greatly impact the overall speed and performance of the computer system.

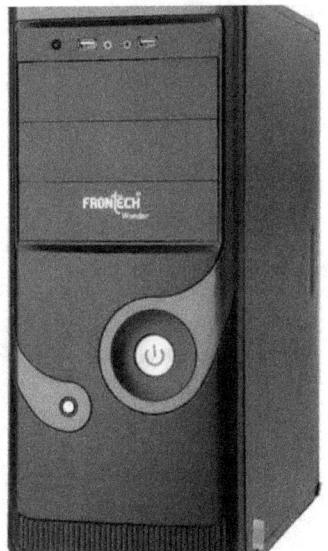

Central processing Unit (CPU)

3. **Random Access Memory (RAM)**: RAM is the temporary storage area that the CPU uses to store data and instructions that it needs to access quickly. It acts as a bridge between the CPU and the storage devices, allowing for faster data retrieval and execution.

Random Access Memory (RAM)

4. **Hard Disk Drive (HDD) or Solid-State Drive (SSD)**: The HDD or SSD is used for long-term storage of data and programs. The HDD uses rotating magnetic disks, while the SSD uses flash memory to store data. SSDs are generally faster and more reliable than HDDs.

HDD vs SSD

5. **Graphics Processing Unit (GPU):** The GPU is responsible for rendering images, videos, and graphics on the computer screen. It enhances the performance of graphics-intensive tasks such as gaming, video editing, and 3D modeling.

Graphics Processing Unit (GPU)

6. **Power Supply Unit (PSU):** The PSU provides electrical power to the computer system. It converts the main AC power supply into DC power that is used by all the components in the computer.

Power Supply Unit (PSU)

7. **Cooling System**: Computer components generate heat during operation, and a cooling system is used to dissipate this heat and prevent overheating. It typically includes fans, heat sinks, and sometimes liquid cooling systems.

Computer Cooling System

8. **Expansion Cards**: These are additional cards that can be inserted into expansion slots on the motherboard to enhance the capabilities of the computer. Examples include networking cards, sound cards, and graphics cards.

Expansion Cards

9. **Cables and Connectors**: Various cables and connectors are used to connect the internal components together and to peripheral devices. This includes cables for power, data transfer, and audio/video connections.

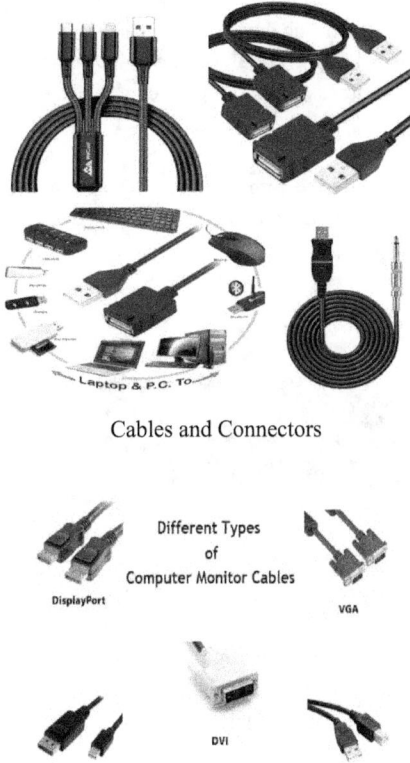

Cables and Connectors

Computer Peripheral devices and their connections

Peripheral devices are external devices that can be connected to a computer to expand its functionality or provide input/output capabilities. These devices connect to the computer via various cables and connectors to enhance the functionality and usability of a computer system. Understanding their connections and compatibility is essential for proper setup and usage. Some common peripheral devices and their connections include:

1. **Keyboard**: Keyboards are the primary input devices for computers. They typically connect to the computer through a USB port or a PS/2 port.

A keyboard

2. **Mouse**: The mouse is another input device that allows users to control the movement of the cursor on the computer screen. It can connect to the computer via a USB port or a PS/2 port.

A mouse

3. **Monitor**: Monitors or displays are output devices that provide visual output from the computer. They usually connect to the computer through an HDMI, DVI, or VGA port, depending on the available ports on the computer and the monitor.

A Monitor

4. **Printer**: Printers are output devices that allow you to print text, images, and documents from a computer. They can be connected to a computer via USB, Ethernet, or wireless connections.

A printer

5. **Scanner**: Scanners are input devices that allow you to digitize physical documents, photos, or images and save them on your computer. They are typically connected to the computer via a USB port.

A scanner

6. **Speakers**: Speakers are output devices that provide audio output from the computer. They can connect to the computer through a 3.5mm audio jack, USB port, or wirelessly via Bluetooth.

A set of speakers

7. **External Hard Drive**: External hard drives can be connected to a computer to provide additional storage space. They usually connect via a USB or Thunderbolt port.

External Hard Drive

8. **Webcam**: Webcams are input devices that capture video and audio, allowing users to communicate or record videos. They typically connect to the computer via a USB port.

A piece of webcam

9. **Microphone**: Microphones are input devices that capture audio. They can be connected to a computer via a 3.5mm audio jack or USB port.

Microphone

10. **Game Controllers**: Game controllers, like joysticks, gamepads, or racing wheels, connect to computers to control gameplay. They can connect via USB, Bluetooth, or specialized gaming ports.

Game Controllers

11. **Network Adapter**: Network adapters, such as Ethernet cards or Wi-Fi adapters, enable the computer to connect to wired or wireless networks. They connect via Ethernet cables or wireless connections like Wi-Fi.

Network Adapter

12. **USB Hub**: USB hubs expand the number of available USB ports on a computer, allowing you to connect multiple USB devices simultaneously. They connect to the computer via a USB port.

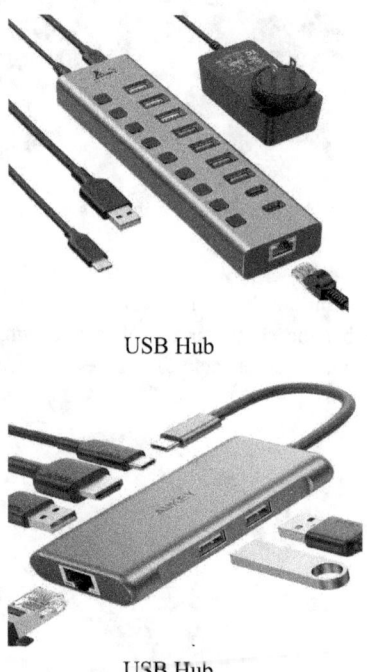

USB Hub

USB Hub

Computer Keyboard and keys

The computer keyboard is an input device that allows users to type, enter commands, and interact with various programs and applications. It consists of several different keys, each designed for specific functions. Here is an extensive overview of the various keys on a standard computer keyboard and their functions:

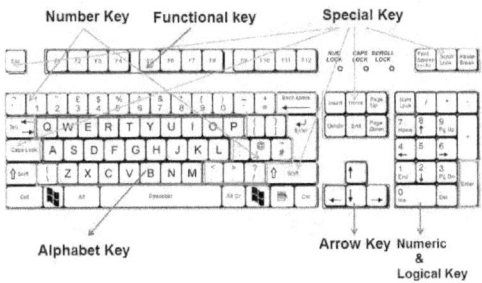

Fig: Computer Keyboard Keys

1. **Alphanumeric Keys:**
   These keys include letters (A-Z) and numbers (0-9). They are used for typing text and entering alphanumeric characters.

2. **Function Keys (F1-F12):**
   Function keys perform different actions depending on the software or application being used. Common uses include accessing help menus, opening settings, and executing specific actions within programs.

3. **Modifier Keys:**
   Ctrl (Control Key): Used in combination with other keys to trigger specific commands or keyboard shortcuts.

4. **Alt (Alternate Key):**
   Used in combination with other keys to access additional functionality or navigate menus.

5. **Shift Key**:
   Used to type capital letters or access secondary characters on keys.

6. **Windows Key (or Command Key on Mac)**: Opens the Start Menu or Start Screen on Windows, used for various system commands.

7. **Navigation Keys**:
   Arrow Keys: Used to move the cursor or selection up, down, left, or right within documents, spreadsheets, or other interfaces.

8. **Home/End Keys**:
   Moves the cursor to the beginning or end of a line or document.

9. **Page Up/Page Down Keys**:
   Scrolls the document or webpage up or down one page at a time.

10. **Insert/Delete Keys**:
    Inserts or deletes characters at the cursor's current position.

Editing Keys:

11. **Backspace Key**:
    Deletes the character before the cursor.

12. **Enter/Return Key**: Adds a new line or executes a command.

13. **Tab Key**: Indents text or moves between fields or elements in a form.

14. **Numeric Keypad**:
    Located on the right side of many keyboards, it functions as a dedicated calculator-like numeric input. It includes numbers, mathematical operators, and additional functions (e.g., Num Lock, Enter/Return).

Special Keys:

15. **Esc (Escape Key):** Used to cancel or exit operations or menus.

16. **Print Screen/SysRq Key**: Captures a screenshot of the current screen.

17. **Scroll Lock**: Historically used to control scrolling within documents or spreadsheets.

18. **Pause/Break Key**: Pauses the execution of a program or command.

Media Keys:

19. **Play/Pause, Stop, Next Track, Previous Track**: Controls media playback on the computer.
20. **Volume Control Keys**: Adjust the volume level.

21. **Mute Key**: Toggles sound on/off.

Keyboard Function keys

Function keys, often labeled as **F1 to F12,** are located on the top row of a computer keyboard. These keys serve different functions depending on the operating system and the software being used. These keys can also be programmed by software developers to perform specific functions within their applications. It's therefore important to check the application's documentation or settings to determine the specific functionality of the function keys within that program.

Here is a general overview of the common uses of function keys:

F1: Often used as the "Help" key. Pressing F1 can provide context-sensitive help or open a help menu for the currently active program.

F2: Frequently used for renaming files or folders. Pressing F2 when a file or folder is selected allows you to quickly change its name.

F3: Typically used to open a search feature within the current application or operating system. In Windows, pressing F3 opens the search feature in many programs and the Explorer file manager.

F4: In Windows, commonly used to open the address bar in a web browser or to open the search feature within a program. In some applications, like Microsoft Excel, it can repeat the last action.

F5: Often used to refresh or reload a webpage or file. Pressing F5 in a web browser or some other programs will refresh the current content.

F6: Frequently used to move the focus to different areas of an open application or interface, such as the address bar in a web browser or different panes within a program.

F7: Sometimes used for checking spelling and grammar in word processing programs or opening the caret browsing feature in web browsers.

F8: Commonly used during the boot process of a Windows computer to access the advanced boot options. It may also be used in specific programs for various functions.

F9: The function key's purpose varies based on the software or operating system being used. It doesn't have a standard universal function.

F10: Generally used to activate menu bar options in many applications. In Windows, pressing F10 can also activate the menu bar of an open program.

F11: Often used to toggle between full-screen and regular view mode in web browsers. It can also be used in other applications to switch to a full-screen display.

F12: Often used to open the "Save As" dialog box in many applications. In web browsers, it can display the developer console for inspecting web elements.

Keyboard short-cut keys and their functions

Shortcut keys, also known as hotkeys or keyboard shortcuts, are combinations of keys that perform specific actions or commands. These shortcuts allow users to perform tasks more quickly and efficiently without relying solely on the mouse or touch-based interactions. Learning and utilizing shortcut keys can significantly speed up workflow, increase efficiency, and, ultimately enhancing the overall computing experience

Here is an extensive overview of some commonly used shortcut keys and their uses:

1. **Copy, Cut, and Paste**:

    Ctrl + C: Copy selected text or item.
    Ctrl + X: Cut selected text or item (removes it from its current location).
    Ctrl + V: Paste copied or cut text or item.

2. **Undo and Redo**:

    Ctrl + Z: Undo the last action.
    Ctrl + Y: Redo the last action.

3. **Save and Open**:

    Ctrl + S: Save the current document or file.
    Ctrl + O: Open a new document or file.

4. **Select and Deselect**:

    Ctrl + A: Select all text or items within the current document or window.
    Ctrl + D: Deselect any selected text or items.

5. Zoom In and Zoom Out:

Ctrl + + (Plus Key): Zoom in to enlarge the content or text.
Ctrl + - (Minus Key): Zoom out to reduce the size of the content or text.
Ctrl + 0 (Zero Key): Reset the zoom level to 100%.

6. Find and Replace:

Ctrl + F: Open the find dialog box to search for specific text or content.
Ctrl + H: Open the replace dialog box to find and replace specific text or content.

7. Print:

Ctrl + P: Open the print dialog box to print the current document or file.

8. Task Management:

Alt + Tab: Switch between open applications or windows.
Ctrl + Alt + Delete: Open the task manager for Windows to manage running processes and applications.
Command + Space: Opens Spotlight search on Mac to quickly search for files, applications, and perform system tasks.

9. Web Browsing:

Ctrl + T: Open a new tab in web browsers.
Ctrl + W: Close the current tab in web browsers.
Ctrl + R: Refresh the current webpage.
Ctrl + D: Bookmark the current webpage.

10. File Navigation:

Windows Key + E: Open File Explorer (Windows) or Finder (Mac) to browse files and folders.
Ctrl + N: Open a new file explorer or Finder window.

11. Text Formatting:

Ctrl + B: Bold selected text.
Ctrl + I: Italicize selected text.
Ctrl + U: Underline selected text.

12.   Window Management:

Windows Key + D: Show or hide the desktop.
Windows Key + L: Lock the computer.
Windows Key + Arrow Keys: Snap the current window to the left, right, top, or bottom of the screen..

The Computer Mouse

The computer mouse is an essential peripheral device that allows users to interact with graphical user interfaces (GUIs) by controlling the movement of a cursor or pointer on a computer screen. It is a versatile tool that enables precise navigation and selection of objects, making it an integral part of modern computing..

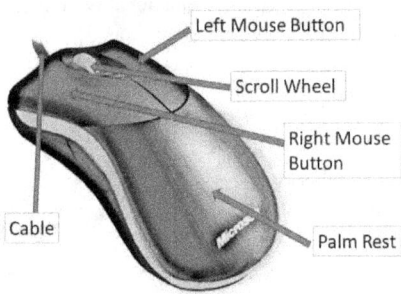

A simple labeled mouse

Types of Computer Mice

1. **Mechanical Ball Mouse**: The mechanical ball mouse is the oldest and most straightforward type of mouse. It consists of a rubber or plastic ball that rolls when the mouse moves. The internal mechanism detects the motion of the ball and translates it into cursor movement on the screen. Mechanical ball mice require a mouse pad for optimal functionality and tend to accumulate dirt and dust over time, leading to decreased accuracy.

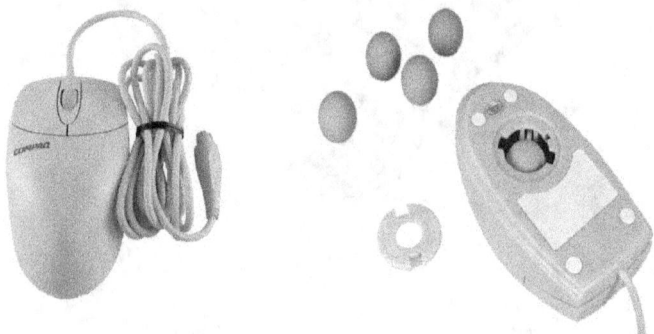

Mechanical ball mice

2. **Optical Mouse**: Optical mice use a light-emitting diode (LED) or laser to track movement. The underside of the mouse contains a sensor that captures images of the surface, and the reflected light is analyzed to determine the cursor's position. Optical mice are more precise than mechanical ball mice and do not require a mouse pad. Additionally, they are less prone to dust accumulation.

An Optical mouse

3. Wireless Mouse: A wireless mouse eliminates the need for a physical connection to the computer. It uses radio frequency (RF) signals, Bluetooth, or infrared technology to communicate with a receiver connected to the computer. Wireless mice offer greater freedom of movement and declutter the workspace. They are powered either by batteries or rechargeable batteries and require periodic charging or battery replacement.

A wireless mouse

4. **Trackball Mouse**: A trackball mouse features a stationary mouse body with a built-in ball on the top surface. Instead of moving the entire mouse, users rotate the trackball using their fingers or thumbs to move the cursor. Trackball mice are useful in situations where there is limited space for mouse movement, and they can reduce strain on the wrist since the entire device does not need to be moved.

A Trackball Mouse

5. Touchpad: A touchpad is a built-in input device commonly found on laptops and some keyboards. It functions by detecting finger movements across its surface. Users can perform various gestures, such as tapping, scrolling, and swiping, to control the cursor and interact with the interface. Touchpads are compact and do not require additional desk space like external mice. They provide a convenient input method for laptop users when a mouse is not readily available.

A Touchpad

Tips for Using a Computer Mouse

1. **Positioning**: Place the mouse within easy reach, with your forearm resting comfortably on the desk. Keep your wrist in a neutral position to minimize strain and prevent repetitive stress injuries.

2. **Grip**: Hold the mouse with a relaxed grip, using your fingertips and thumb on the buttons. Avoid gripping the mouse too tightly, as this can lead to fatigue and discomfort.

3. **Movements**: Move the mouse using your forearm and shoulder rather than just your wrist. This helps prevent wrist strain and promotes smoother and more precise movements.

4. **Button Usage**: The left button is the primary button used for clicking and selecting. The right button is often used to access context menus or perform secondary functions. Familiarize yourself with the mouse's scroll wheel, which allows you to navigate through documents and web pages quickly.

5. **Customization**: Many mice offer customizable buttons and programmable functions. Take advantage of software provided by the manufacturer to tailor the mouse's settings to your preferences and workflow, such as adjusting sensitivity, assigning shortcuts, or creating macros.

6. **Regular Maintenance**: Clean the mouse regularly, especially for mechanical ball mice that tend to accumulate dirt and dust. Use a cotton swab or microfiber cloth to remove debris from the sensor area of optical mice. For wireless mice, replace or recharge batteries as necessary to ensure uninterrupted functionality.

7. **Mousepad Usage**: While mechanical ball mice require a mouse pad for optimal tracking, optical and laser mice can work on various surfaces. However, using a good quality mouse pad can enhance precision and reduce wear and tear on the mouse feet, leading to smoother movements.

Computer Graphical User Interface (GUI)

The graphical user interface (GUI) of a computer is the visual interface that allows users to interact with the operating system and applications. It consists of various sections and elements that provide a user-friendly and intuitive way to navigate, access, and manipulate computer resources. Let's explore the different sections of a typical GUI in detail:

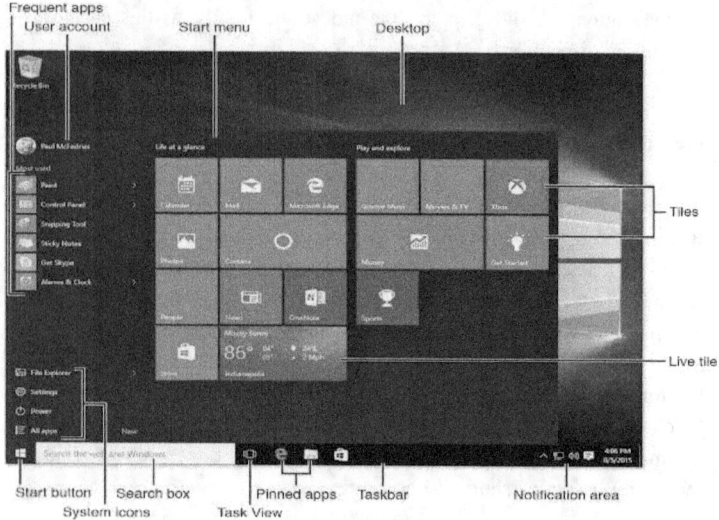

A labeled Graphical User Interface

Desktop:

The desktop is the main area that appears when the computer boots up or when the user logs in. It serves as a workspace where users can place icons, folders, and files for easy access. The desktop often includes a wallpaper or background image, which can be customized according to the user's preferences.

Taskbar:

The taskbar is a horizontal or vertical bar typically located at the bottom or side of the screen. It is a prominent feature of the GUI and provides quick access to essential tools, applications, and system settings. The taskbar typically includes the Start button (in Windows) or the Launchpad (on macOS), which allows users to access the main menu or application launcher.

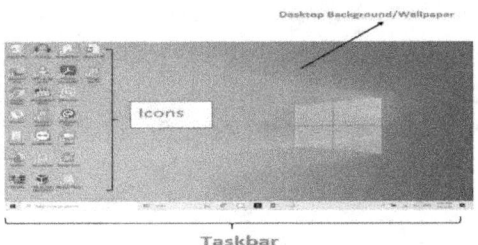

Start Menu/Launchpad:

The Start menu (in Windows) or Launchpad (on macOS) is a menu system that provides access to installed applications, documents, system settings, and search functionality. It is a central hub for launching applications, navigating the file system, and accessing system utilities and tools.

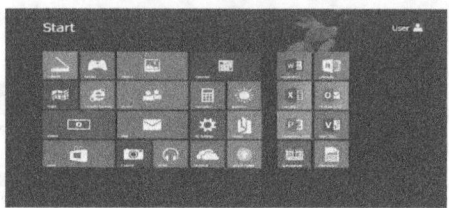

Window Management:

GUIs allow multiple applications or windows to be open and displayed simultaneously. The window management section of the GUI provides features for controlling and organizing these windows. This includes minimizing, maximizing, and resizing windows, as well as moving them around the screen. Windows can be arranged side by side, cascaded, or tiled to optimize productivity and multitasking.

Title Bar:

The title bar is located at the top of each window and displays the name of the application or document being viewed. It also contains control buttons for minimizing, maximizing, or closing the window. The title bar may also include additional options, such as the ability to pin a window on top or access a window's context menu.

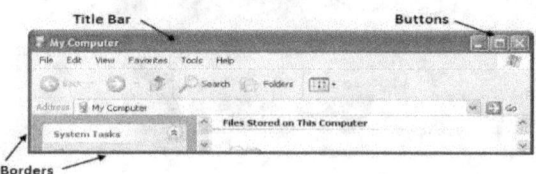

Menu Bar:

The menu bar is typically located below the title bar and provides a hierarchical list of menus for accessing various functions and features of an application. Each menu contains a set of commands, which can be accessed by clicking on them. The menu bar often includes standard menus such as File, Edit, View, Tools, and Help, each containing specific options related to the application's functionality.

Toolbars:

Toolbars are additional graphical elements located below or above the menu bar that provide quick access to frequently used functions or tools. They consist of icons or buttons representing specific actions, such as save, print, copy, paste, and formatting options. Users can interact with these icons or buttons to perform tasks more efficiently.

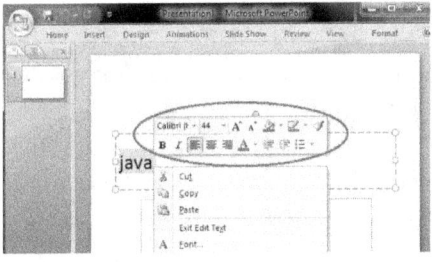

Navigation Pane/Sidebar:

The navigation pane, also known as the sidebar, is a section typically located on the left or right side of the screen. It provides easy navigation and access to different areas of the operating system or applications. The navigation pane can display shortcuts to frequently accessed folders, bookmarks, file directories, or options to switch between different views or modes.

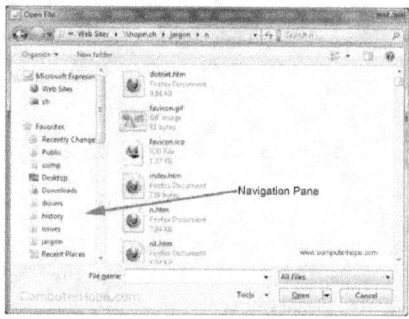

Status Bar:

The status bar is located at the bottom of an application window and provides information about the current state or progress of a task. It may display details such as the number of pages in a document, the word count, or the status of a file transfer. The status bar can also show notifications, system messages, or display icons for active processes or services.

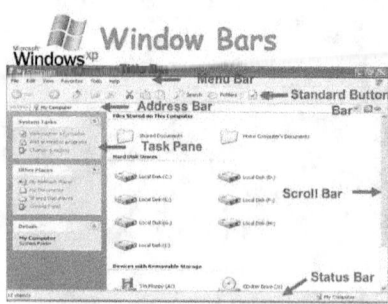

Dialog Boxes:

Dialog boxes are temporary windows that prompt users for input or provide specific information or options. They can be used for tasks such as opening or saving files, setting preferences, confirming actions, or displaying error messages. Dialog boxes typically contain buttons, checkboxes, dropdown lists, and text fields for user interaction.

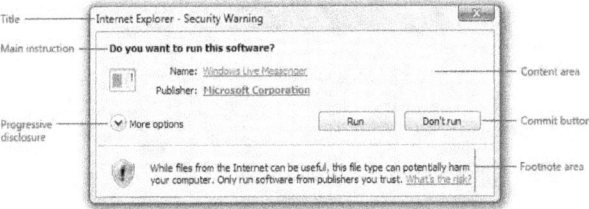

Context Menus:

Context menus, also known as right-click menus, are popup menus that appear when the user right-clicks on an element such as a file, folder, or an area of the interface. Context menus provide a context-sensitive list of options relevant to the selected item. These options can include actions like renaming, copying, deleting, or opening properties.

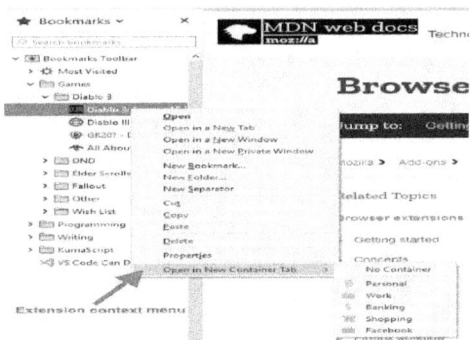

Notifications and System Tray:

Notifications, often displayed as small popup windows, inform users about significant events, updates, or alerts. They can appear outside of the main application window to prevent interruption of the user's workflow. The system tray, located in the taskbar, displays icons representing running applications, background processes, notifications, and system utilities.

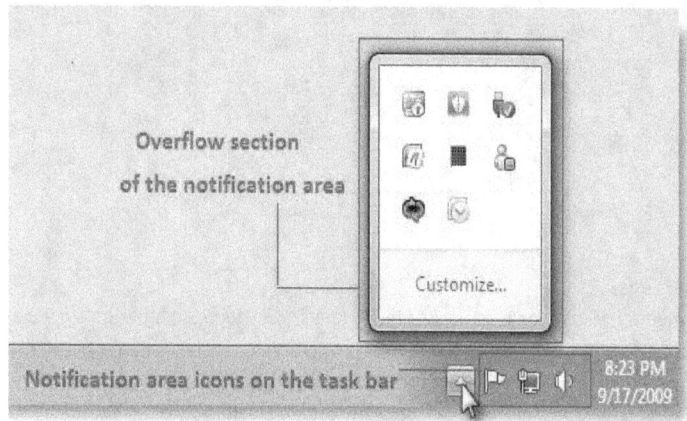

How to boot the computer

The specific steps to boot a computer may vary slightly depending on the computer's manufacturer and the operating system installed. Additionally, if the computer uses Secure Boot or has a boot menu, the process may involve additional steps. It's recommended to consult the computer's manual or manufacturer's instructions for detailed guidance on booting the specific computer model.
However, To boot a computer, follow these general steps:

A. Power on the computer by pressing the power button.
B. The computer will start a Power-On Self-Test (POST) to check its hardware components.

C. After the POST, the computer's Basic Input/Output System (BIOS) or Unified Extensible Firmware Interface (UEFI) will initialize the hardware and perform system checks.

D. The computer will then attempt to boot from a specified boot device, usually the internal hard drive.

E. If the boot device is successfully found and contains a valid operating system, the computer will load the operating system into memory.

F. The operating system will then start its initialization process and display the login or user interface screen.

How to turn off the Computer

To turn off a computer system, you can follow these step-by-step instructions:

Save your work:
Before shutting down the computer, make sure to save any unsaved documents or projects to prevent data loss.

Close open applications:
Close all the open applications and programs on your computer. You can do this by clicking the 'X' button in the upper right corner of each window, or by going to File > Close or Exit.

Close any background processes:
Some applications may run background processes that you might not see on the screen. Make sure to close or exit those processes as well. You can do this by right-clicking on the application icon in the taskbar or system tray and selecting 'Exit' or 'Close'.

Disconnect from the internet (optional):
If you're connected to the internet via Wi-Fi or Ethernet, you may want to disconnect before shutting down. This is not necessary but can be useful in specific situations.

Save your settings:
Some applications, such as text editors or design software, may have a 'Save Settings' option. It's a good idea to save your custom settings If you have made any changes that you want to keep.

Click on the 'Start' button:
On Windows, click on the 'Start' button located in the bottom left corner of the screen. On macOS, click on the Apple logo in the top left corner of the screen.

Choose the 'Power' or 'Shut Down' option:
In the Windows Start menu, click on the power button icon. A menu will appear with options such as 'Shut Down', 'Restart', 'Sleep', or 'Hibernate'. Select the 'Shut Down' option to turn off the computer. On macOS, click on the 'Shut Down' option from the drop-down menu that appears after clicking the Apple logo.

Confirm the shut down:
In Windows, you may be prompted to confirm the shut down by clicking 'Shut down' again. On macOS, a dialog box will appear asking if you want to save your work. Make sure to save any remaining work and click 'Shut Down' to proceed.

Wait for the computer to turn off:
After confirming the shut down, wait for a few moments as the computer completes the shutdown process. You may see a screen indicating the progress of shutdown or a spinning wheel on macOS.

Power off the computer:
Once the computer has fully shut down, you can proceed to power it off completely. For desktop computers, press and hold the power button until the system powers off. For laptops, simply pressing the power button once should turn off the device.

Troubleshooting common hardware issues

It is important to note that some hardware issues may require replacement or repair of the faulty component. In such cases, it is advisable to consult a professional technician or the manufacturer for further guidance. However, When troubleshooting common hardware issues, there are a few steps you can take to identify and resolve the problem.

1. **Check Connections**: Ensure that all cables and connections are secure. Sometimes, an issue can be as simple as a loose cable or an improperly connected device. Check the cables and reseat them if necessary.

2. **Restart the Computer**: A simple restart can fix many common hardware problems. Restart your computer and see if the issue persists. This can help resolve temporary glitches or conflicts.

3. **Update Drivers**: Outdated or incompatible drivers can cause hardware issues. Check the manufacturer's website for the latest drivers for your hardware devices. Install the updated drivers and see if the problem persists.

4. **Run Hardware Diagnostics**: Many computers have built-in hardware diagnostic tools that can help identify and resolve hardware issues. Run these diagnostics to scan for any problems and follow the recommended actions to fix them.

5. **Test Hardware on Another Computer**: If possible, connect the hardware device to another computer to see if the issue persists. This can help determine if the problem lies with the hardware itself or with the computer's configuration.

6. **Check for Overheating**: Overheating can cause hardware malfunctions. Ensure that your computer's cooling system is functioning properly. Clean any dust or debris from fans and vents, and monitor the temperature of your hardware components using software tools if available.

7. **Scan for Malware**: Malware infections can cause hardware issues or interfere with the normal functioning of hardware devices. Run a thorough antivirus and malware scan to check for any infections. Remove any detected malware and see if the problem is resolved.

8. **Check Power Supply**: If the issue involves the power supply, ensure that it is connected properly and supplying adequate power to the hardware devices. Test the power supply on a different outlet or use a different power cord if available.

9. **Check for Compatibility Issues**: Ensure that the hardware device is compatible with your computer's operating system and hardware configuration. Check the system requirements and compatibility documentation provided by the manufacturer.

10. **Seek Professional Help**: If you have tried all the above steps and the issue still persists, it may be time to seek professional help. Contact the manufacturer's support team or a reputable computer repair service for assistance in diagnosing and resolving the hardware issue.

Simple Computer Maintenance Guide

Computer maintenance is essential for ensuring your computer runs smoothly and remains in good working condition. Regular maintenance helps prevent problems, optimize performance, and prolong the lifespan of your computer. Here are some key areas of computer maintenance:

Software Updates: Keeping your operating system, applications, and antivirus software up to date is crucial. Updates often include security patches and bug fixes, reducing the risk of malware infections and improving overall system stability and performance.

Disk Cleanup: Regularly clean up your computer's hard drive by removing unnecessary files and temporary data. This can be done using built-in disk cleanup tools or third-party software. Deleting temporary files, clearing browser caches, and removing old downloads can free up valuable storage space and improve system responsiveness.

Disk Defragmentation: Over time, files on your hard drive can become fragmented, affecting read and write speeds. Running a disk defragmentation program can rearrange files, making them contiguous and improving disk performance. However, modern operating systems often handle disk fragmentation automatically, so manual defragmentation may not be necessary.

Scan for Malware: Running regular malware scans using reputable antivirus or anti-malware software helps detect and remove any malicious programs that may be affecting your computer's performance or security. Ensure your antivirus software is up to date and perform full system scans on a regular basis.

Hardware Cleaning: Dust accumulation inside your computer can impede airflow and cause overheating. Periodically clean the fans and vents using compressed air or a soft brush to remove dust and ensure proper cooling. Be cautious when cleaning the internal components and refer to manufacturer guidelines if needed.

Software Cleanup: Uninstalling unnecessary programs can help free up system resources and improve performance. Use the built-in control panel or specialized software to remove unused or unwanted applications. Also, remove any browser extensions or plugins that are no longer needed.

Backup and Recovery: Regularly backing up your important files and data is crucial in case of hardware failure, malware infection, or accidental deletion. Create multiple backups and store them in different locations to protect your data. Test the backup restoration process occasionally to ensure it's working correctly.

Keep Hardware in Good Condition: Handle your computer and its components with care. Avoid placing it in dusty or humid environments, install surge protectors, and use the appropriate power supply to prevent electrical damage. Additionally, ensure proper ventilation to prevent overheating.

By regularly performing these maintenance tasks, you can optimize your computer's performance, improve its reliability, and extend its lifespan. Additionally, consider consulting with professionals for specialized maintenance or repair needs, especially for complex hardware issues or software troubleshooting.

Introduction to Programming

Programming is the process of creating instructions or programs that can be executed by a computer to perform specific functions or tasks. It involves writing, testing, and debugging code to produce software applications or programs.

Programming languages serve as a means of communication between humans and computers. They provide a structured way to express algorithms and solve problems by breaking them down into smaller, manageable steps. Different programming languages offer different syntax and capabilities, allowing developers to choose the most suitable language for their project.

Programming is not limited to computer software development; it also extends to areas such as web development, mobile app development, artificial intelligence, and data analysis. Understanding programming concepts and having coding skills can open up various career opportunities in the technology industry.

Key Concepts and Terminologies:

Algorithms: Algorithms are step-by-step procedures or instructions for solving a problem. They form the basis of programming, helping developers design logical and efficient solutions.

Syntax: Syntax refers to the rules and guidelines for writing code in a specific programming language. Each programming language has its own syntax, which determines how statements, expressions, variables, and other elements are written. Syntax errors occur when code violates the rules of the language.

Keywords: Keywords are reserved words in a programming language that serve predefined purposes and cannot be used as variable names. Examples of keywords include "if," "else," "for," "while," and "function." Different languages may have different sets of keywords

Variables: Variables are named storage locations used to hold values or data. They can be assigned values, modified, and used in calculations or comparisons within a program.

Data Types: Data types define the kind of data that can be stored in a variable. Common data types include integers, floating-point numbers, strings, characters, Boolean values, and arrays.

Control Flow: Control flow refers to the order in which instructions or statements are executed within a program. Control flow structures like conditional statements (if-else, switch) and loops (for, while) determine the flow and direction of program execution.

Operators: Operators are symbols or keywords used to perform operations on data, such as arithmetic operations (+, -, *, /), logical operations (&&, ||), comparison operations (>, <, ==), and assignment (=). Operators have precedence rules that determine the order in which operations are executed.

Functions: Functions are reusable blocks of code that perform specific tasks. They encapsulate a set of instructions and can be called multiple times from different parts of the program.

Libraries and Frameworks: Libraries and frameworks are collections of pre-written code or modules that provide additional functionality to programming languages. They allow programmers to leverage existing code to solve common problems quickly. Libraries contain reusable code, while frameworks provide a structure or foundation for building applications.

Documentation and Community Support: Programming languages often have extensive documentation and community support. Documentation includes official guides, tutorials, and references, while community support includes online forums, Q&A sites, and developer communities. Developers can refer to documentation and seek help from the community when learning or encountering problems.

Classes and Objects: Object-oriented programming (OOP) utilizes classes and objects to represent and manipulate real-world entities. A class serves as a blueprint for creating objects, which are instances of that class. OOP allows for code reuse, modularity, and easier maintenance.

Debugging: Debugging is the process of identifying and fixing errors or bugs in a program. Debugging tools and techniques help programmers detect and resolve issues to ensure the program functions correctly.

Programming Languages

There are numerous programming languages available, each with its strengths and weaknesses. Some popular programming languages include:

Python: Python is a versatile and beginner-friendly language known for its simplicity and readability. It is widely used in various domains, including web development, data analysis, machine learning, and scientific computing.

JavaScript: JavaScript is primarily used for web development and is supported by all modern web browsers. It enables dynamic and interactive features on websites, such as animations, form validation, and user interface enhancements.

Java: Java is a general-purpose programming language that runs on the Java Virtual Machine (JVM). It is often used for building desktop applications, enterprise-level software, Android apps, and server-side development.

C++: C++ is a powerful and efficient language commonly used for system-level programming, game development, and high-performance applications. It blends object-oriented and low-level programming, providing control over system resources.

Ruby: Ruby is known for its simplicity and elegant syntax. It is commonly used in web development frameworks like Ruby on Rails to create dynamic websites and web applications.

Learning to program requires patience, practice, and a logical mindset. It is recommended for beginners to start with a beginner-friendly language and gradually expand their knowledge by learning new concepts and languages.

Basics of Python as a programming languages

Python is a high-level, interpreted programming language that emphasizes code readability and simplicity. It was created by Guido van Rossum and first released in 1991. Here are the basics of Python as a programming language:

Syntax: Python has a clean and readable syntax, which makes it easy to understand and write code. Indentation is used to define blocks of code instead of using braces or keywords. Python code is structured in a way that encourages readability and reduces unnecessary complexity.

Readability: Python aims to have code that is simple to read and understand. It uses English keywords rather than punctuation, which makes it more accessible for beginners or non-programmers to learn and read Python code.

Dynamic Typing: Python is dynamically typed, which means that variable types are determined at runtime. Variables do not need to be declared with a specific data type, and their type can be changed during the execution of the program. This provides flexibility but can also lead to potential type-related errors.

Interpreted Language: Python is an interpreted language, which means that Python code is executed line by line by the Python interpreter rather than being compiled into machine code beforehand. This makes the development process quicker, as there is no need for a separate compilation step.

Extensive Libraries and Modules: Python has a large standard library that provides a wide range of pre-built modules and functions covering various functionalities. These libraries and modules enhance the capabilities of Python and allow developers to write efficient code without reinventing the wheel.

Object-Oriented Programming (OOP): Python supports object-oriented programming, allowing developers to create and use classes, objects, and inheritance. OOP helps in organizing code, promoting reusability, and structuring complex programs into manageable units.

Pythonic Idioms: Python follows a set of conventions and idioms known as "Pythonic" code. Pythonic code is characterized by its simplicity and readability. Writing Pythonic code is considered good practice and helps improve code maintainability.

Versatility: Python is a versatile language that can be used for various purposes, including web development, data analysis, machine learning, scientific computing, scripting, and automation. It has become increasingly popular in these domains due to its ease of use and extensive libraries.

Integrated Development Environments (IDEs): Python has several IDEs and text editors with dedicated support for Python development. Popular IDEs include PyCharm, Visual Studio Code, and Spyder. These tools provide features like code autocompletion, debugging, and project management, enhancing the development experience.

Community Support: Python has a robust and active community of developers who contribute to its growth. The Python community regularly releases updates, packages, and frameworks, making it easier for developers to find solutions, support, and resources. Python's popularity ensures a wealth of online resources, tutorials, and forums for learning and troubleshooting.

Python's simplicity, readability, and strong community support have contributed to its growing popularity. It is widely used in various industries and is an excellent language for beginners to start their programming journey with. With its versatile applications and numerous libraries, Python continues to be a favored choice for developers worldwide.

Basics of Java as a programming languages

Java is a high-level, object-oriented programming language that was developed by Sun Microsystems (acquired by Oracle Corporation) and first released in 1995. Here are the basics of Java as a programming language:

Syntax: Java has a C-like syntax, making it familiar to programmers from the C/C++ background. It uses braces to define blocks of code, and semicolons to separate statements. Java code must be written within classes and methods.

Object-Oriented Programming (OOP): Java is a strongly object-oriented language, emphasizing the use of classes and objects. It follows the principles of encapsulation, inheritance, and polymorphism. OOP allows for code reusability, modularity, and ease of maintenance.

Platform Independence: Java programs, once compiled into bytecode, can run on any platform that has a Java Virtual Machine (JVM). This platform independence is achieved by compiling the Java source code into bytecode, which is then interpreted and executed by the JVM.

Automatic Memory Management: Java uses automatic garbage collection to manage memory. Developers do not need to manually allocate or deallocate memory, as the JVM handles memory management tasks such as memory allocation and deallocation.

Exception Handling: Java provides a robust exception handling mechanism, allowing developers to catch and handle exceptions that may occur during program execution. This helps in writing resilient and error-free code.

Standard Library: Java has an extensive standard library that provides a wide range of classes and methods for various functionalities. From basic input/output operations to advanced networking and database handling, the standard library offers many pre-built components that simplify coding.

Multithreading and Concurrency: Java supports multithreading, allowing developers to run multiple threads of execution concurrently within a single program. This enables efficient utilization of system resources and enables the development of responsive and concurrent applications.

Security: Java has built-in security features that protect against common security vulnerabilities. The Java Security Manager and sandboxing capabilities allow developers to run untrusted code in a restricted execution environment, enhancing the overall security of Java applications.

Networking and Distributed Computing: Java provides extensive support for networking and distributed computing. The Java API includes classes and interfaces for socket programming, remote method invocation (RMI), and Java Messaging Service (JMS), making it easy to develop networked and distributed applications.

Rich Ecosystem: Java has a vast ecosystem of frameworks, libraries, and tools that extend its capabilities. Popular frameworks like Spring, Hibernate, and JavaFX make development more streamlined and efficient. Additionally, the large Java community offers a wealth of resources, tutorials, and support for developers.

Java's platform independence, strong OOP support, automatic memory management, and robust standard library have made it a popular choice for developing various applications including enterprise software, mobile apps, web applications, and more. Its versatility, coupled with its extensive ecosystem, contributes to its widespread adoption and longevity in the programming world.

Writing and executing simple programs

To write and execute a simple Java program, you'll need a **text editor** to write the code and a **Java Development Kit (JDK)** installed on your computer to compile and run the program. Here's a step-by-step guide:

Step 1: Install the Java Development Kit (JDK)

Go to the Oracle website: https://www.oracle.com/java/technologies/javase-jdk11-downloads.html Download and install the appropriate JDK version for your operating system.

Step 2: Set up the Java Development Environment

Set the PATH environment variable to include the JDK's "bin" directory.
For Windows:
Open the system properties (Win + Pause/Break).
Go to "Advanced System Settings".
Click on the "Environment Variables" button.
Under "System Variables", select the "Path" variable and click on the "Edit" button.
Add the path to the JDK's "bin" directory to the list of paths.
For macOS:
Open a terminal.
Enter the command: nano ~/.bash_profile .
Add the following line at the end:

export PATH="/Library/Java/JavaVirtualMachines/jdk-11.0.x.jdk/Contents/Home/bin:$PATH"
Save the file (Ctrl + O) and exit (Ctrl + X).

For Linux:
Open a terminal.
Enter the command: sudo nano /etc/environment .
Add the following line at the end:

PATH="/usr/local/sbin:/usr/local/bin:/usr/sbin:/usr/bin:/sbin:/bin:/usr/games:/usr/lo
cal/games:/usr/lib/jvm/jdk-11.0.x/bin"
Save the file (Ctrl + O) and exit (Ctrl + X).
Verify your JDK installation by running the following command in a terminal:
java -version

Step 3: Write a Simple Java Program

Open a text editor and create a new file with a ".java" extension. For example,
"HelloWorld.java".
In the file, write the following code:

```
public class HelloWorld {
    public static void main(String[] args) {
        System.out.println("Hello, world!");
    }
}
```

Step 4: Compile and Run the Java Program

Open a terminal and navigate to the directory where you saved the Java program.
Compile the program by running the following command: javac HelloWorld.java
If there are no errors, a compiled bytecode file called "HelloWorld.class" will be
generated.
Run the program with the following command: java HelloWorld
You should see the output: "Hello, world!"

Congratulations! You've successfully written and executed a simple Java program.
You can now experiment with more complex programs or explore the various
features of the Java language.

DEBUGGING

Debugging and problem-solving techniques are essential skills for developers and IT professionals. When faced with software bugs or technical issues, these techniques help identify and resolve problems effectively. Here are some key techniques to consider:

Reproduce the Issue:

One of the first steps in debugging is to reproduce the issue consistently. Understand the sequence of actions or inputs that trigger the problem. This enables you to isolate and analyze the specific conditions leading to the error.

Divide and Conquer:
If the problem is complex or not immediately apparent, break it down into smaller parts. Divide the system or code into smaller components to identify the root cause. Focus on debugging one component at a time instead of trying to analyze the entire system.

Use Debugging Tools:
Utilize debugging tools provided by development environments, such as integrated development environments (IDEs) or debuggers. These tools offer features like breakpoints, variable inspection, step-by-step execution, and stack traces to help identify issues.

Logging and Instrumentation:
Use logging mechanisms throughout your code to track program flow, variable values, and error messages. This helps track the execution path and provides valuable information when analyzing issues. Instrumentation libraries or frameworks can simplify this process.

Analyze Error Messages:
Carefully investigate error messages or exceptions thrown by the software. Error messages often contain useful information about the nature of the problem and its location. Understand the specific message and its context to pinpoint the issue.

Experiment and Iterate:
Try various solutions or changes to the code and observe the results. Sometimes, changing a particular line of code or configuration can bring a quick resolution. Be systematic and document your changes to learn from the debugging process.

Check Inputs and Assumptions:
Review your code to ensure that inputs and assumptions are correct. Validate user inputs, data formats, or API responses to avoid unexpected behavior or errors. Incorrect assumptions about inputs can often lead to bugs or unexpected results.

Seek Collaboration and External Help:
If you're stuck and unable to find a solution, don't hesitate to seek help from colleagues or online developer communities. Engaging in discussions or asking specific questions can provide fresh perspectives and possible solutions.

Practice a Scientific Approach:
Debugging requires a methodical approach. Formulate hypotheses about the problem, conduct experiments, and analyze the results. Learn to observe, collect data, and make informed decisions based on the evidence at hand.

Continuous Learning:
Finally, debugging is a skill that improves with experience and continuous learning. Stay updated with new technologies, development best practices, and debugging techniques. Regularly analyze and reflect on your debugging processes to refine your problem-solving skills.

Remember that debugging can be a time-consuming process, and patience is crucial. Develop a systematic approach, stay organized, and document your findings and solutions. With practice and persistence, you'll become a proficient debugger capable of tackling even the most challenging issues.

Data Structures and Algorithms

Data Structures and Algorithms are fundamental concepts in computer science and programming. They are crucial for designing efficient and scalable solutions to various computational problems. Let's dive into the basics of data structures and algorithms:

Data Structures:

A data structure is a way of organizing and storing data in a computer's memory. It defines the relationships between the data elements and the operations that can be performed on them. Some commonly used data structures include:

1. Arrays: A collection of elements stored at contiguous memory locations. Arrays provide constant-time access to elements but have a fixed size.

2. Linked Lists: A sequence of nodes where each node contains data and a pointer to the next node. Linked lists allow dynamic size and efficient insertion/deletion but have slower access times.

3. Stacks: A Last-In-First-Out (LIFO) data structure. Elements can only be inserted or removed from the top of the stack.

4. Queues: A First-In-First-Out (FIFO) data structure. Elements can only be added at the rear and removed from the front.

5. Trees: A hierarchical data structure with a root node and child nodes. Trees are used for representing hierarchical relationships and implementing various algorithms such as binary search.

6. Graphs: A set of vertices/nodes connected by edges. Graphs are used to represent relationships between objects and provide solutions to problems like shortest path, network connectivity, and more.

Algorithms:

An algorithm is a step-by-step procedure or set of rules for solving a problem. It takes input, follows a series of well-defined steps, and produces the desired output. Algorithms can be categorized based on their efficiency and complexity. Some important algorithms include:

1. Sorting Algorithms: Sorting algorithms arrange elements in a specific order, such as ascending or descending. Examples include bubble sort, insertion sort, merge sort, quicksort, and heapsort.

2. Searching Algorithms: Searching algorithms find the location or existence of a target element within a data structure. Common algorithms include linear search, binary search (for sorted data), and hash-based search.

3. Graph Algorithms: Graph algorithms solve problems related to graphs, such as finding the shortest path (Dijkstra's algorithm), traversing all nodes (Depth-First Search and Breadth-First Search), and detecting cycles (Tarjan's algorithm).

4. Dynamic Programming: Dynamic programming solves complex problems by breaking them down into overlapping subproblems and efficiently reusing solutions. This technique is often used for optimization problems or problems that can be divided into smaller, overlapping subproblems.

5. Divide and Conquer: This technique involves breaking a problem into smaller subproblems, solving them independently, and then combining their solutions to find the overall solution. Examples include merge sort, binary search, and quicksort.

The choice of data structure and algorithm depends on the problem at hand and the specific requirements such as time complexity, space complexity, and performance considerations. It is essential to analyze and understand the problem before selecting the correct data structure and algorithm.

Proficiency in data structures and algorithms is highly valued in the software industry. It allows software engineers to develop more efficient and optimized code, resulting in faster applications and better user experiences. Regular practice, reading books, solving coding challenges, and participating in coding competitions are effective ways to improve your knowledge and skills in data structures and algorithms.

Introduction to computer networks and the internet

Computer networks and the Internet play a crucial role in connecting devices and facilitating the exchange of information and resources worldwide. They have revolutionized the way we communicate, work, and access information. Let's explore the basics of computer networks and the Internet:

Computer Networks:

A computer network is a collection of interconnected devices, such as computers, servers, switches, routers, and wireless access points, that are linked together to enable communication and data sharing. Network devices are interconnected using various mediums, including wired (Ethernet cables) and wireless (Wi-Fi) connections.

Types of Networks:

Local Area Network (LAN): A LAN is a network that covers a small geographical area, such as a home, office building, or campus. LANs allow devices to share resources and communicate with each other at high speeds.

Wide Area Network (WAN): A WAN is a network that extends over a large geographical area, connecting devices across cities, countries, or continents. The Internet is the most prominent example of a WAN, enabling global connectivity.

Metropolitan Area Network (MAN): A MAN is a network that covers a larger geographical area, typically a city. It provides high-speed connectivity for organizations and institutions within a specific metropolitan area.

Wireless Networks: Wireless networks use radio waves to connect devices without the need for physical cables. Wi-Fi networks are the most common type of wireless networks, enabling mobile devices to access the Internet and communicate with other devices.

The Internet

The Internet is a global network of networks that connects millions of devices worldwide. It is a decentralized network, meaning it does not have a single point of control or ownership. Instead, it is made up of interconnected networks operated by various Internet Service Providers (ISPs), organizations, and individuals.

Key Concepts of the Internet:

Protocols: The Internet relies on a set of protocols, including the Transmission Control Protocol (TCP) and Internet Protocol (IP), to ensure reliable communication and data transfer between devices. These protocols define rules for addressing, routing, and transmitting data packets.

IP Addressing: Each device connected to the Internet has a unique IP address. IP addresses allow devices to identify and communicate with each other. IPv4 (32-bit) and IPv6 (128-bit) are the two major versions of IP addresses.

Domain Name System (DNS): DNS translates human-readable domain names (e.g., www.example.com) into IP addresses. It acts as a distributed directory system, allowing users to access websites and services using easy-to-remember domain names.

World Wide Web (WWW): The World Wide Web is a collection of interconnected web pages and resources accessible through the Internet. It uses the Hypertext Transfer Protocol (HTTP) for transmitting webpages and resources and is accessed through web browsers.

Internet Security: With the growth of the Internet, ensuring security and privacy has become crucial. Technologies like firewalls, encryption (SSL/TLS), and Virtual Private Networks (VPNs) are used to protect data and secure communications over the Internet.

The Internet has revolutionized various aspects of our lives, including communication, education, e-commerce, entertainment, and more. From sending emails to streaming videos, conducting online transactions to accessing information, the Internet has become an essential part of our digital world.

Network Protocols and Architectures:

Network protocols and architectures play a crucial role in enabling communication and data transfer between devices in a computer network. They provide a framework for organizing and standardizing the way devices interact and exchange information. Let's explore some key network protocols and architectures:

TCP/IP:
The Transmission Control Protocol/Internet Protocol (TCP/IP) is the foundational protocol suite of the Internet. It defines a set of rules and procedures for transmitting data packets across networks. TCP ensures reliable, ordered, and error-free delivery of data, while IP handles addressing and routing of packets. TCP/IP has become the standard protocol suite for most computer networks, facilitating seamless communication between devices.

Ethernet:
Ethernet is a widely used network technology for local area networks (LANs). It defines the physical and data link layer specifications for wired communication. Ethernet uses a system of frames to transmit data over cables, employing protocols such as Ethernet II and IEEE 802.3. It provides high-speed, low-cost, and reliable communication within LANs.

Wi-Fi:
Wi-Fi (Wireless Fidelity) is a wireless network technology based on the IEEE 802.11 standards. Wi-Fi allows devices to connect to a network without the need for physical cables. It uses radio waves to transmit data between devices and access points. Wi-Fi networks provide mobility and flexibility for users to connect their devices wirelessly, enabling access to the Internet and local resources.

DNS:
The Domain Name System (DNS) is a protocol and distributed database system that translates human-readable domain names into IP addresses. DNS enables users to access websites and services using easy-to-remember domain names (e.g.,

www.example.com) instead of complex IP addresses. DNS works in a hierarchical manner, with DNS servers resolving domain names to their corresponding IP addresses.

HTTP and HTTPS:

The Hypertext Transfer Protocol (HTTP) is the protocol used for transmitting web pages and resources over the Internet. HTTP defines how clients (web browsers) and servers communicate, allowing users to access websites and retrieve information.

HTTPS (HTTP Secure) is an extension of HTTP that uses encryption (SSL/TLS) to secure the transmission of data. It ensures confidentiality and integrity of data exchanged between the client and server, essential for secure browsing and online transactions.

OSI Model:

The Open Systems Interconnection (OSI) model is a conceptual framework that standardizes the functions and protocols of computer networks. It consists of seven layers, each responsible for specific tasks related to network communication. The layers include Physical, Data Link, Network, Transport, Session, Presentation, and Application. The OSI model helps in understanding the various protocols and their interactions in a structured manner.

IP Addressing:

IP addressing is a fundamental aspect of network protocols and architectures. Each device connected to a network, including the Internet, is assigned a unique IP address. IP addresses allow devices to identify and communicate with each other. The most commonly used IP version is IPv4, which uses 32-bit addresses. However, the transition to IPv6, with 128-bit addresses, is happening to accommodate the growing number of connected devices.

Network protocols and architectures provide the foundation for reliable and efficient communication across computer networks.

Basic network configuration and troubleshooting

It is important to know that these (network configuration and Troubleshooting) are important skills for network administrators and individuals who manage computer networks. Let's explore some key concepts and techniques related to network configuration and troubleshooting:

1. **IP Address Configuration:** IP address configuration is a crucial step in setting up a network. It involves assigning unique IP addresses to devices connected to the network. IP addresses can be configured manually (static IP) or automatically (dynamic IP) using protocols like DHCP (Dynamic Host Configuration Protocol). Proper IP address configuration ensures that devices can communicate with each other and access network resources.

2. **Subnetting**: Subnetting is the process of dividing a large network into smaller subnetworks or subnets. It helps in efficient management and organization of IP addresses within a network. Subnetting involves determining the subnet mask, which specifies the network and host portions of an IP address. Proper subnetting ensures proper routing of data and prevents network congestion.

3. **Network Topology:** Network topology refers to the physical or logical layout of a network. Popular network topologies include bus, star, ring, and mesh. Understanding the network topology helps in identifying potential bottlenecks, troubleshooting connectivity issues, and planning network expansion.

4. **Network Devices Configuration:** Configuration of network devices, such as routers, switches, and firewalls, is essential for proper network operation. This includes setting up device IP addresses, setting up VLANs (Virtual Local Area Networks), configuring routing protocols, enabling firewall rules, and implementing security measures. Proper device configuration ensures smooth network operation and enhances network security.

5. **Troubleshooting Connectivity Issues**: When network connectivity issues arise, troubleshooting becomes crucial. Some common steps for troubleshooting connectivity issues include:

    a. Physical Check: Ensure all cables and connections are properly connected and undamaged.

    b. Ping Test: Use the ping command to test connectivity between devices. Ping can help identify if a device is reachable or if there is a network issue.

    c. IP Configuration Check: Verify the IP address, subnet mask, and default gateway settings of devices to ensure they are correctly configured.

    d. DNS Check: Verify DNS settings to ensure proper resolution of domain names to IP addresses.

    e. Firewall Check: Check firewall settings to ensure they are not blocking necessary network traffic.

    f. Network Device Check: Validate the configurations of routers, switches, and other network devices to ensure they are functioning properly.

    g. Network Traffic Analysis: Use network monitoring tools to analyze and capture network traffic to identify any anomalies or bottlenecks.

6. Security Configuration: Configuring network security measures is paramount to protect against unauthorized access and data breaches. This includes setting up firewalls, implementing access controls, enabling encryption (e.g., HTTPS), and regularly updating firmware and software to patch security vulnerabilities.

7. Documentation and Network Diagrams:

Keeping accurate documentation and network diagrams is crucial for troubleshooting and managing a network efficiently. Documenting IP addresses, subnetting, device configurations, and network topology helps in troubleshooting issues and managing network changes effectively.

By understanding the basics of network configuration and troubleshooting, network administrators and individuals can ensure the smooth functioning of computer networks, identify and resolve connectivity issues promptly, and implement necessary security measures.

Introduction to cybersecurity

Cybersecurity has become a critical aspect of modern-day technology and information systems. With the increasing reliance on digital platforms and the proliferation of cyber threats, understanding the fundamentals of cybersecurity has never been more important. This introduction will provide a brief overview of cybersecurity, its importance, and key concepts within the field.

What is Cybersecurity?
Cybersecurity refers to the practice of protecting computer systems, networks, and data from unauthorized access, disruption, or damage. It involves implementing measures and technologies to safeguard information and technology assets, preventing cyber attacks, and mitigating the potential impact of breaches.

Why is Cybersecurity Important?
Cybersecurity plays a crucial role in protecting sensitive information, ensuring the privacy of individuals and organizations, and maintaining the integrity and availability of systems and networks. Cyber attacks can result in financial loss, reputational damage, data theft, and even impact critical infrastructure. By implementing robust security measures, organizations can mitigate risks, maintain trust with customers, and safeguard their digital assets.

Key Concepts in Cybersecurity:

1. Threats and Attacks: Understanding the types of threats and attacks is fundamental in cybersecurity. This includes malware (such as viruses, worms, and ransomware), phishing, hacking, social engineering, DDoS attacks, and insider threats. Each type of attack poses different risks and requires specific countermeasures.

2. Vulnerabilities: Vulnerabilities are weaknesses or flaws in systems, networks, or applications that cyber attackers can exploit. Identifying and

patching vulnerabilities is crucial for maintaining a secure environment. Regular security assessments, vulnerability scanning, and updates are essential to stay ahead of potential threats.

3. Risk Management: Risk management involves identifying potential risks, assessing their impact and likelihood, and implementing strategies to mitigate or reduce risks. This includes evaluating the cost-benefit of security measures, implementing security controls, and creating incident response plans.

4. Authentication and Access Control: Authentication ensures that only authorized individuals or systems can access resources, such as networks, systems, or sensitive data. Strong passwords, multi-factor authentication, and access control policies are commonly employed to prevent unauthorized access.

5. Encryption: Encryption involves transforming sensitive information into a unreadable format, which can only be deciphered with a decryption key. Encryption provides confidentiality and ensures data integrity during transmission and storage. It is particularly important for securing sensitive data, such as financial transactions and personal information.

6. Security Awareness and Training: Humans remain one of the weakest links in cybersecurity. Educating employees and users about cyber threats, best practices, and security protocols is crucial. Regular cybersecurity training can help prevent common mistakes and reduce the likelihood of successful attacks.

7. Incident Response and Recovery. Despite robust security measures, breaches can still occur. Having an incident response plan in place is vital to minimize the damage, contain the breach, and restore systems and data. Timely detection, response, and recovery are key to reducing the impact of a breach and returning to normal operations.

As technology continues to advance and cyber threats become increasingly sophisticated, cybersecurity plays a vital role in protecting information and systems. By understanding the key concepts and implementing best practices, individuals and organizations can enhance their security posture and mitigate the risks associated with cyber attacks. Investing in cybersecurity is essential to safeguard intellectual property, maintain customer trust, and ensure the stability and safety of digital infrastructure.

Protecting networks and systems from threats and attacks

This is a critical aspect of cybersecurity. By implementing robust security measures and adopting best practices, organizations can significantly reduce the risk of unauthorized access, data breaches, and other cyber threats.

Here are some key strategies and technologies for safeguarding networks and systems:

1. **Firewall**: A firewall acts as a barrier between a trusted internal network and untrusted external networks, such as the internet. It monitors and controls incoming and outgoing network traffic based on predefined security rules, ensuring that only authorized traffic is allowed.

2. **Intrusion Detection and Prevention Systems (IDPS):** IDPS are designed to detect and prevent unauthorized access, attacks, and malicious activities on networks and systems. These systems monitor network traffic, analyze events, and take action based on predefined rules or anomaly detection.

3. **Secure Configuration**: Ensuring that networks, operating systems, and applications are configured securely is crucial. This involves disabling unnecessary services, implementing strong password policies, regularly patching systems, and using up-to-date software versions to mitigate known vulnerabilities.

4. **Network Segmentation**: Splitting a network into smaller segments or subnetworks can help limit the impact of a successful attack. By segregating resources and implementing access controls, an organization can contain or prevent the lateral movement of attackers within its network.

5. **Intrusion Prevention System (IPS)**: IPS complements the firewall by actively searching for and blocking potential malicious activity on a network. It analyzes network traffic in real-time, detects known attack patterns, and blocks or mitigates the attacks.

6. **Antivirus and Anti-malware Software**: Deploying antivirus and anti-malware solutions help identify and remove malicious software, such as viruses, worms, and Trojans. Regularly updating the antivirus software and scanning systems for threats is essential to maintain an effective defense.

7. **Vulnerability Management**: Proactively identifying and addressing vulnerabilities in systems and networks is critical. This involves conducting regular vulnerability assessments, deploying patches and updates, and staying informed about newly discovered vulnerabilities.

8. **Monitoring and Logging**: Implementing robust monitoring and logging systems allows organizations to detect and analyze suspicious activities. By monitoring network traffic, system logs, and security events, organizations can identify potential threats and respond promptly.

9. **Regular Backups**: Regularly backing up critical data and system configurations is crucial for recovery in case of a successful attack. Offsite backups and testing of restoration processes can help ensure the availability and integrity of data.

10. **User Education and Awareness**: Educating users about security best practices, such as strong password management, recognizing phishing emails, and avoiding suspicious downloads or websites, is essential. Regular security awareness training can help reduce the risk of human error compromising the network.

By implementing a combination of these strategies and technologies, organizations can enhance their network and system security, reducing the risk of threats and attacks. Additionally, staying informed about the latest security threats, updates, and industry best practices is essential to stay ahead of emerging threats and maintain a strong defense.